My Journey from the Plantation, through the Courts, to Mediation

❖❖❖❖❖

Pauline Ravenall

TEACH Services, Inc.
P U B L I S H I N G
www.TEACHServices.com ● (800) 367-1844

Copyright © 2022 Pauline Ravenall
Copyright © 2022 TEACH Services, Inc.
ISBN-13: 978-1-4796-1465-3 (Paperback)
ISBN-13: 978-1-4796-1466-0 (ePub)

All Scripture quotations, unless otherwise indicated, are taken from the King James Version. Public domain.

TEACH Services, Inc.
P U B L I S H I N G
www.TEACHServices.com ● (800) 367-1844

Words of Praise...

"If ever there were a story of desire, determination, and dedication to be the best one can be no matter what the obstacles, it is the autobiography of Pauline Barnes Ravenall. *My Journey from the Plantation, through the Courts, to Mediation* is written by a woman who doesn't share secrets easily. However, in this book she reveals her private struggles from sheltered isolation to international welcome.

"Pauline comes across in her memoirs as who she truly is—a humble personality, heroic fighter, and honorable servant of God. You will be surprised, delighted, and inspired!"

— Dr. Calvin B. Rock, former Vice President, General Conference of Seventh-day Adventists

❖❖❖

"I've known Pauline Ravenall for many years. You will find her story to be quite interesting and faith building.

"Her desire to honor God in hr sphere of influence is a reminder to brighten the corner where we are."

~ Pastor David A. Long. Southern Union Conference of SDA

Table of Contents

CHAPTER 1

I was born to my parents, Will Barnes Sr. and Vanessa Hayes-Barnes, on a sharecropper plantation in Macon County, in the town of Montezuma, Georgia. My parents both were of average height. Both parents were God-fearing. They lived what they believed to be right. We do better as we learn better. I never remember knowing my father attending a church service; I saw my mother in church once. Although my parents didn't attend church, they were honest in what they did, and it was from the heart. Going to church does not necessarily make a person God-fearing.

We (their children) were required to attend Sunday school with a cousin, W.D. Bass (he was a deacon in the Travels Rest Baptist Church), walking to the country church (approximately six miles) each third Sunday of each month (church service was only held once a month). There was Sunday school before the divine service. I vividly remember a Bible verse on the picture flip chart:

"I was glad when they said unto me, Let us go into the house of the LORD" (Ps. 122:1).

My father was one of twenty-four children. My mother was the youngest of thirteen children. When I first saw my grandparent from both sides of my family I was preschool age—about five years old. We had to travel to the rural areas of Macon County, Georgia. Though I only saw them once, I have vivid memories of my grandmothers. My mother's mother, Frances

I was born to my parents, Will Barnes Sr. and Vanessa Hayes-Barnes, on a sharecropper plantation in Macon County, in the town of Montezuma, Georgia.

Hayes, was ill at the time and sick, lying in bed. I remember sitting quietly, observing the situation, and listening to the adults talk around me. My father's mother, Mary Little, was short in stature, had white hair, and smoked a corncob pipe. I remember her sitting on a stool outside of her house. I'm not sure why I didn't see my grandparents very often. Perhaps it was because of the distance that it took to go see them, but it would have been nice to get to know them a bit better.

Mom and Dad—Willie and Vanessa Barnes

The parents of eight growing children, my father had to always find living accommodations wherever he could for his family. We lived on various plantations, all of which were in Georgia. Our accommodations were typical of country living: wooden framed houses with a tin roof, wooden floors, fireplaces, oil lamps to light the house, iron stoves used with wood to heat the house and cook food. One thing that differed back then was that blacks had no electricity and no inside plumbing, only outside accommodations. It was also only black workers that could be found in the field. This was all I knew. Plantation work could be exhausting, but we worked hard and played hard whenever the opportunity presented itself.

My Mom with Eight Children—Frances, Annie, Geneva, Pauline, Mae, Willie, Bernice, and Louise

We were seven girls and one boy, with only two older girls to work (their names were Mary Frances Barnes-Johnson—named for both grandparents—and Annie Mae Barnes-Keaton). The third child, Geneva, was the babysitter for the younger siblings. I am the fourth of eight children and at this time was not of school age. I was around six years old. There were four younger siblings. As of this writing, all of my sisters are now passed away. Only my brother and I remain. My first school I attended was Culpepper School. It was a one-room, one-teacher school in a framed building located in a wooded area, near a dirt road in the countryside. It was the only school for all the grades. Mrs. Ingram was the teacher. One memory I have of her was in the classroom. I remember standing, facing the blackboard. I didn't know which was my right hand and which was my left. Mrs. Ingram said, "Pauline, your right hand is the one at the end of the blackboard." Since that time, I always, whenever I am in doubt, I visualize standing at the blackboard with my right hand at the end of the blackboard, and I can tell which hand is right and which hand is left. I have always had a desire to learn more and wondered why things were different in families and communities from which we lived—especially in the white communities. It seemed that, in the other communities, they didn't have to work as much as I did.

As far back as I can remember, my parents provided a good life for our family—plenty of work and plenty of food. We had a lot of outdoor activities when the weather provided too much rain to work in the fields. My childhood activities were work, feeding the animals, playing hopscotch, and hide-and-go-seek. Houses in the country were built high off the ground, so the children would run and play under the house. When the weather was dry, we had to work from sunup to sundown. When lunchtime rolled around, the beginning of it was signaled by the sounding of a bell, and it ended as it started—with the ring of a bell—exactly one hour from the beginning to the end of lunch. When it was time for lunch, we just looked for a place in the shade to sit and eat lunch at the end row. The row might have been cotton, peanuts, or whatever.

> *As far back as I can remember, my parents provided a good life for our family—plenty of work and plenty of food. We had a lot of outdoor activities when the weather provided too much rain to work in the fields.*

We were lucky if there were trees for shade so that we could escape the sun if only for that brief time while eating. Sometimes, when there was no bell, time was told by the shadow of the sun over your body—your shadow told you the time of day. Work began long before the "paid" work and lasted long after. Before and after a hard day's work, we had animals to care for. We had to feed and gather eggs from the chickens, milk the cows, feed the hogs and mules, and take care of other critters. Although I didn't have a favorite animal, I enjoyed caring for them.

Because I was always misbehaving, causing problems with my older sister (Geneva) who was the babysitter to our younger siblings, my mother decided to take me to work with her in the fields—whether it was picking cotton, picking up peaches, shaking peanuts, and the like. I worked alongside her. Adult wages were $2.00 per day. A child's salary was $0.50. I worked all day for $0.50. This was prior me being old enough to attend school. Even after working all day, I didn't have a lack of energy. We were very healthy. We ate all natural foods and pure water—nothing like today's diet. Imagine a garden that could provide all manner of fresh fruits and vegetables as well as corn from the fields that would be ground into cornmeal for breads and other things. We had fresh milk from the cows and what would today be called "organic, free-range eggs" right from our very own chickens. Our food was abundant and straight from nature, unlike the highly processed and unhealthy foods that are so easy to buy at the grocery store today.

It seems that even if it rained during the week, Saturdays were always dry. So, when it was permissible, we could work on Saturday mornings and, unlike during the wages made during the week, receive the entire $0.25 (half a day's wage) for ourselves. I would save my money until our biweekly or monthly trips when we went to town on the wagon with our father to sell his produce.

These trips were exciting because now I could buy whatever I wanted. Usually, I would buy material with pretty prints on it so I could make my own clothes. I often would look through the store window to see the white (Caucasian) ladies always dressed in white blouses and blue skirts and wondered why I did not have the same nice clothing.

Most times, my father would give the produce away for little or no money in exchange for alcohol. He was a very generous person, a good provider for our family, and a very hard worker. My father was a giver, a provider for those in need who could not provide for themselves. We had so much—more than we needed—and my father, with his caring heart, would rather give the excess away to those who needed it rather than making a few more pennies for himself This is what I believe is God-fearing, generosity straight from the heart.

When it was too wet to do farm work, many times my father would be found with his ax in hand and his burlap sack over his back going to cut down the white man's trees or whatever work he could find to do. When he returned, most times, he would have leftover food such as fresh beef bones or other bones that were given him with a little meat on them. Then he would use fresh vegetables from our garden to make soup for the family. Maybe it was the barter system or maybe he was being repaid for his own generosity. I can never remember going hungry. Not only did we have the produce from our gardens and milk and eggs from the animals, but my father would bring home squirrels, rabbits, opossums, and the like. We were hardly ever sick. If we were ever sick, my parents would go out in the woods to get herbs for teas for our ailments. Back then people didn't just run to a drugstore to pick up a medication; knowledge of medicinal herbs was passed from parent to child and natural means were used in healing. If only we still had that knowledge and connection to nature and history today maybe people would live a healthier, more robust life as we did.

We were sharecroppers, and an unfortunate aspect of life back then was the reliance the black sharecroppers were required to have on the white landowners. A sharecropper would be given credit for seed, tools, even living quarters, and after the harvest would receive a share of the value minus any charges the landowner had him pay. During the week of work, the pay went to our mother or the plantation owners. We never knew if we had cleared our debt because, at the end of the year, the owner/foreman would always tell my father that he would have to remain for another year because he did not clear anything. According to the owner, the charges to my father and our family were not covered by the crops we brought in and sold. Not being present (or allowed) to be at the closing of yearly books, sharecroppers only took the white owner's word. If the white owner said you did not clear/profit anything and you need to stay another year to make up the difference, the blacks had to stay if there were no other choices available. Most times there were no other choices.

We always knew when our mother was very unhappy about something. She and our father would argue, she would gather us up, and we would walk along the roadside to one of her sisters' houses—even at night. This happened many times. It was always the same sister (Aunt Pommie Lee Mason) that took us in. Once we arrived at her home—regardless of the time of night—she never failed to open her door and immediately go into her kitchen and begin to place wood in her stove, then put on her apron, light a fire, and cook a full meal for my mother and her children. Afterward, she would prepare a place for us to sleep. I never knew her to attend a church service, but I believe she was a Christian from the heart just as I believe my father was, giving away his produce to the ones that could not afford to pay. Christ knows the heart, and living a life of care for others just as He would is what being a Christian is all about.

Eventually, my parents separated. My father went to live with his sister (Aunt Susie Locket) in Ft. Valley, Georgia. My two oldest sisters (Mary Frances and Annie Mae), along with our youngest preschool age baby sister Louise, relocated to Orlando, Florida. I'm not sure why my baby sister was sent with my older sisters, but maybe it was because she was not yet school age and the rest of the family would be following them to Florida soon after. My next older sister got married at a very young age. She moved in with her husband and his parents and siblings. Therefore, since all of my siblings had moved on and moved out, I had no one to walk to school with me anymore and I could not continue the walk to attend school alone. It was not safe. My mother permitted me to go and live with a first cousin (Nora Thompson) and her family so I could walk to school with her children. This left my two younger sisters and our only brother with my mom. Soon thereafter, my oldest sister (Mary Frances) sent someone for us to come live in Orlando, Florida. This was very different since all I had known, up to this point, was country living! Eventually, all our family relocated to Florida.

During the year, we girls would pull up a certain kind of grass with long roots and pretend it was hair. We would put the top part of the grass in a pop bottle to support the "hair" and use the roots for hair to wash and braid. This is how we learned to style human hair.

When I was maybe eight years old, I remember getting my one and only ever commercial doll in my entire life—a doll without hair. Maybe that was to make it look more like a baby. The doll had to be protected from water, otherwise the doll's paper or paper-like skin covering would peel off. Imagine putting something with a paper label on it in water to soak the label off. When it got wet, the paper would easily peel right off. It didn't matter though—I was just happy to have a doll to play with! At Christmastime, we (the children) would get a shoe box each with fruit, nuts, red peppermint candy canes, and the like. No toys. By living in the country on plantations (along with other families with children), we learned to create toys and games to play with. Of course, the dolls we made had grass for hair, and the neighbor children would help make clothes for our dolls. The boys would take tin cans, fill them with dirt, and run a wire from one end to the other and then run with them to make noise. One game we all played was hide and seek. The houses were built high off the ground (as homes near beaches often are), therefore we could run under the house, through the fields, all with bare feet, and never get injured.

However, there was very little time for play. There was always work to be done with the animals and field work. Plus, we were tasked with taking care of the foreman's garden and my father's garden and other needed chores. After Christmas, the doll would be wrapped and put away for the next Christmas. The rest of the year, we were busy with chores and other activities, and we didn't have time to play with the doll.

During the year, we girls would pull up a certain kind of grass with long roots and pretend it was hair. We would put the top part of the grass in a pop bottle to support the "hair" and use the roots for hair to wash and braid. This is how we learned to style human hair. Later in life, when I went to live in Orlando, I enrolled in Jones High Vocational School in Cosmetology studies where I was a student. I was more advanced in styling hair than my associates because of my playing with grass roots for hair.

My high school (Jones High School) offered vocational classes along with regular classes. I selected cosmetology simply because other subjects were not familiar to me. My experience with the grass in the bottle in the country had more than prepared me to press and curl real hair in the real world. The late Mrs. Carolyn Clark was the best and only instructor at the school of cosmetology. If a student did not roll the hair correctly around the curling iron, she would take a brush and flatten the hair out and that meant you, the student, would have to begin again to make the perfect curl. I really loved her and her professionalism. After finishing my training, I travelled to Tallahassee, Florida, to sit for the state exam. I passed and received my cosmetology license in 1958. I retired my license in May of 2021. I worked in that field from 1958–2020!

There is a reciprocity (relationship) between Florida and Georgia. The state of Georgia agreed with the state of Florida to accept its license rules credentials. So, I could work in either Florida or Georgia without having to do additional training. A blessing? I definitely think so. I believe it was ordained by the Creator God for my benefit. He is a God worth serving!

Our Family, Mother, Children and Grand Children

CHAPTER 2

Upon arriving in Orlando, things were much different than what I was used to. There were electric lights and indoor plumbing. Also different was the fact that I got to ride a school bus to school. After being in Orlando for a while, an older cousin and his wife (childless) asked me to live with them. I was eager to oblige to have my own room and to ride a bus to school. But this, too, was short lived. It was not a good experience. My thinking is that if couples don't have children, then when faced with taking care of one, they may decide (as in my case) that they would really rather be alone. By this time, I was in my early teens.

I went back to live with my eldest sister, Mary Frances, who was now married to Willie James Johnson. My second oldest sister, Annie Keaton, was then married to Joel Keaton. By this time, they both were Seventh-day Adventist. Our father and my two older sisters were baptized on the same Sabbath (he in Ft. Valley, Georgia, by Pastor Ralph Hairston. My two older sisters in Orlando. It was the early 1950s; I don't know the exact date). I learned later that my father (then living in Ft. Valley, Georgia) was walking past the SDA church on a Sabbath morning. As he was passing, the sound of music alerted his attention. Apparently, he stopped to listen. A member of the church invited him in. Not being properly dressed, he promised to return the next Sabbath. The rest is history. My two sisters living in Orlando, Florida, apparently at the time, must have been visiting or studying with someone, and the baptisms were scheduled on the same Sabbaths. Perhaps this was unknown to each until sometime later. Eternity will reveal.

My oldest sister (Mary Frances and her family) lived in a 4-unit duplex upstairs next door to Mr. Jim. Each duplex up and downstairs had equal numbers of rooms. He had three rooms: Front room, middle room, kitchen, bathroom outside off the back porch. The apartments were located on the second floor.

My sister's apartment was crowded. She and her husband, one child, myself, and four other siblings were all competing for space. With my sister's permission, I asked Mr. Jim if he would let me stay in his front room—the middle room door divided the rooms. He was a tall man and very kind. Mr. Jim consented. That meant I would need to walk down the outside stairs, around the house, then up the back stairs to use the bathroom. In today's world, many would consider this to be unsafe, but it was perfectly safe then.

Across the street from the duplex on Paramore Avenue was Eddie's Grill Café, a mom-and-pop family restaurant. There I met my future husband, Norris Ravenall. He was the only child of Lorene Ravenall-Patrick. He was tall, and his kind spirit made an impression on me. His father passed away earlier when he was a young man. I never met him. Norris was a regular at the restaurant at dinner times.

Across the street from the duplex on Paramore Avenue was Eddie's Grill Café, a mom-and-pop family restaurant. There I met my future husband, Norris Ravenall.

Pauline and Husband, Norris

He was employed at Happy P. Leu Botanical Industrial Company as a yard foreman (he ended up working there for more than twenty-five years). As I was attending high school and working, I had little time to do my schoolwork. Norris was kind and assisted me occasionally with my homework in the basic high school subjects. He had completed his education and served his country in the military. I would give him my assignments at dinnertime, and he would return them the following evening. How thankful I am, even now, for his help and care.

Later, after graduating Jones High School, I was baptized by Pastor J. Malcom Phipps, at Mt. Sinai SDA Church in Orlando.

I asked for and was given a job after school and on weekends at Eddie's Grill Café for $9.00 a week, plus tips—which were very few! I was permitted to eat certain foods on the menu. That helped me to survive without use of a kitchen where I lived. This was my first job away from the fields of Macon County, Georgia. From that salary, I paid $4.00 rent and bought school supplies and other miscellaneous things. I used $2.00 to open a savings account. I had been introduced to tithing, so I was also giving ten percent of what I earned to God. Since that time, I have not been penniless. Money has gotten mighty low at times but never penniless. Praise the Lord for His promises.

Later, after graduating Jones High School, I was baptized by Pastor J. Malcom Phipps, at Mt. Sinai SDA Church in Orlando. I was one of more than 100 candidates. I did not particularly embrace the Adventist message at first. I was rebellious, mostly from a lack of understanding and things being different from what I was accustomed to. Like most people, I simply followed tradition. My lack of understanding and lack of searching made me apathetic. I was very pleased, however, when I gained knowledge of Scripture. This was one of my early experiences that showed me how much I desired to learn, for KNOWLEDGE IS FREEDOM. I haven't regretted it since.

CHAPTER 3

Soon thereafter, I went to live with a relative in Bronx, New York. It was not easy living in a large city with no city experiences. Orlando might have been big compared to rural Georgia, but it was nothing like the big city of New York. I had never seen such tall skyscrapers before or experienced the sheer amount of people and traffic all around me. I had to learn to navigate public transportation in the busiest city in America.

Unfortunately, looking for work, riding subways, and catching buses used up all my savings. My cousin (Josie Smith) and I were very close and remain close to this day. She shared her children's piggy banks monies for my subway fares. She was married and the parent of five children. She had a set of identical twins that I had fun with because I could not tell them apart.

Every job I was offered required Sabbath work. I was determined to keep the Sabbath. The employment agent that we would visit each time we went seeking employment said, "Young lady, you are now in New York and need to work, you better accept a job."

Every job I was offered required Sabbath work. I was determined to keep the Sabbath. The employment agent that we would visit each time we went seeking employment said, "Young lady, you are now in New York and need to work, you better accept a job." But God is faithful.

The very last day, the very last money we had, I was sent to Alrae Hotel on 64th Street downtown Manhattan, New York. After talking with the owner, Peggy Ann Kent, she said, "You can have the job." She was the daughter of 20th Century Fox motion pictures president Sidney Raymond Kent in California. She had two caretakers for her personal needs and several dogs. I would be the dogs' caretaker. The youngest dog was my favorite. His name was Otto. He was a small Chihuahua. The owner's name was Peggy Ann Kent. She was very wealthy. I told her I could not work on Saturdays. She said whatever her primary caretaker and I worked out would be fine with her. As Georgia Brown, her primary caretaker, and I talked, Georgia suggested since she goes to church on Sunday and I attend church on Saturday, I could have Fridays and Saturdays off, and she would have Sundays and Mondays off. That job paid more than any of the other jobs I had interviewed for. I remained on that job for the duration of my stay in New York. The late Mrs. Peggy Ann Kent was very generous. When I was ready to return to Orlando, she gave to me my first airplane ride on Eastern Airlines back to Orlando. I was nervous and scared on my first airplane ride, but I endured the flight. I still have my first piece of Starline Vintage luggage that I took with me on that flight: a Samsonite luggage look-a-like. It was expensive at the time. In today's money, it would be around $100.

I enjoyed my time in New York. It was different than the country life I was used to, but it was an exciting experience. Riding subways was a completely different mode of transportation than I was used to. I had to get used to how it worked, but I adjusted quickly. There were so many tall buildings! I wasn't used to being surrounded by skyscrapers. Manhattan is loud. Taxi cabs were continually blowing their horns. It was a totally different life.

CHAPTER 4

Upon returning to Orlando, Norris and I were married and became parents to three children: Brenda Yvette, Derwin Maurice, and LeMar Kevin. Norris was a very kind man. He had a gentle spirit, and he was a loving husband and father. God has blessed me greatly in my husband and children.

Pauline with her Three Children—Daughter Brenda, Oldest Son Derwin, and Youngest Son Kevin

I am thankful that all of my children were able to attend Seventh-day Adventist Christian schools and have grown up to use their education to be independent and self-supporting. They were also each encouraged to play an instrument and it turns out that they are very musically inclined. Brenda played the piano, Derwin the saxophone, and Kevin the trumpet.

To say I am proud of my children is an understatement. Brenda served in the United States Air Force and the United States Coast Guard as well as with the US Postal Service. Derwin also served his country in the United States Army and remains gainfully employed. Kevin is using his tech skills with the Dekalb County Georgia Service Board as their Director of Information Technology. They are my greatest blessing.

During the early 1960s, Mrs. Savannah (Sandy) Robinson invited me to colporteur with her in selling Seventh-day Adventist Christian magazines. It was short-lived. My first day, the first person I asked, the man said no. I realized that was something I did not want to do, so that ended my selling experience.

Mrs. Robinson continued her colporteur work, but, along with me, she enrolled at the Orange County Vocational School for office training.

She had a conflict with one of the instructors when the instructor asked her about how to prepare and eat "hog jowls." That did not set too well with Mrs. Robinson because she did not eat meat. It was not part of her diet. She was polite but direct and immediately clarified the instructor's assumption. It was—and is—thought that if a person is of a certain race or population, that person will do what the population does. Mrs. Robinson is a person of African descent. The instructor assumed (apparently) Mrs. Robinson ate what the people of that population ate. Presently, whenever Mrs. Robinson and I have a conversation, the subject always comes up and we have a hearty laugh!

My mother always instructed her children that everyone is due the time of day. That meant to speak to people. We should speak, whether we receive a response or not. She taught us that if we do the right thing, right will follow. Maybe the "right thing" meant to stay in our place—to keep your mouth shut and never to "know anything." I'm not sure if I followed exactly, but I tried. At this point segregation was still an issue and racial prejudice still affected community relations. Personally I never experienced a problem, but maybe it was because my motto has always been KNOWLEDGE IS FREEDOM and because of that I never felt the need to respond to any negative actions. I had confidence and knew my worth. As the Bible says, "Confidence in an unfaithful man in time of trouble is like a broken tooth, and a foot out of joint" (Prov. 25:19, KJV).

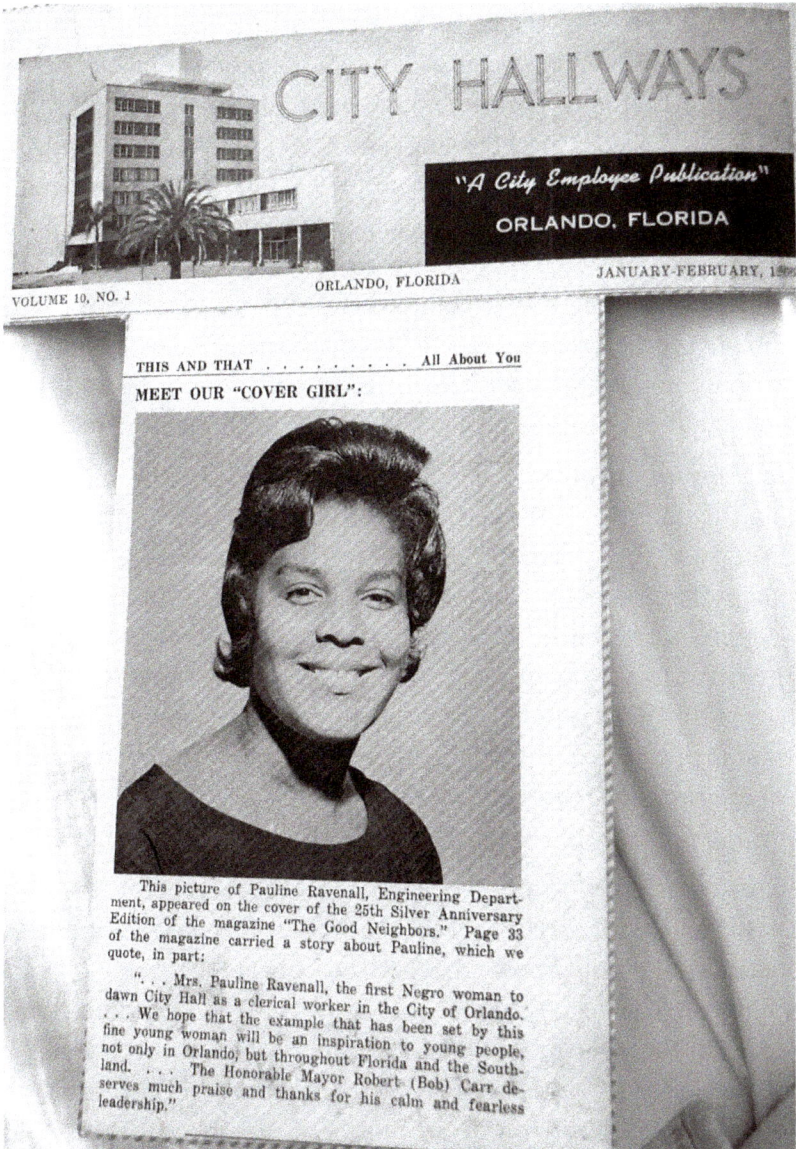

Article about Pauline Being the First African American to Work in City Hall in 100 Years

In July 1964, during the civil rights unrest, the city of Orlando and its city council were looking to place an African American in city hall. The "White Only" racial signs were posted at city hall, but the late Dr. Elaine B. Cox, member of the mayor's council, suggested I be considered for the position as the first black clerical worker to dawn city hall. I was hired. Soon thereafter, the signs were removed. Therefore, I made the city and black community "proud." Like I've said before, KNOWLEDGE IS FREEDOM. It was different than the country way of working. My first assignment was in the Planning and Zoning Department. My second assignment was in the Police Department as an undercover police officer. While the police department was housed in a separate building, I was still part of the now non-segregated city government. Being an undercover officer was an exciting job! I completed police training at the Orlando Police Academy. I carried a weapon, handcuffs, learned arrest procedures, rode in an unmarked vehicle, performed undercover tasks, and helped in stakeout activities in public parks. I also assisted in making arrests.

After my employment was advertised, a radio station named the day "Pauline Ravenall" day. While most people don't have their employment advertised in the newspaper, my situation was different. Such news had not been publicized before and while integration was moving forward and many people supported it, there were still many who were angered at the thought of a black woman working in the city government shoulder-to-shoulder with white people. The following day, a cross was burned and thrown in my front yard overnight. The next morning, my husband moved it out of the yard. I experienced no harm. Even though there were tensions and unrest all around, I never suffered from any personally.

I later transferred to the Engineering Department for a total of ten years with the city of Orlando, Florida. It was the most exciting place to work because of all the knowledge housed between its walls! I so enjoyed learning the functions of an entire city government, and there is a lot to learn. All laws that govern a city are formed within those walls. You can find all the information for street layout, property information, sewers, and park designs there as well. In fact, I set up the entire Engineering Department filing system and had every file, every folder memorized. If someone came in and asked where something was, I could respond with, "It is in file drawer A, in a green folder, with a yellow label" (or any combination of drawers and colors). What is amazing to me is the thought that anywhere you go in the world there has to be a place where the laws of a city are formed and stored, and I was blessed to be able to work in mine. And after my years of service, to leave with my name placed on one of its city streets and city parks was an honor.

THE GOOD NEIGHBORS MAGAZINE

THE FIRST IN 100 YEARS

MRS. PAULINE RAVENALL

Pictured here is Mrs. Pauline Ravenall, the first Negro woman to dawn City Hall as a clerical worker in the history of the City of Orlando which demonstrates the value of the ballot and the reward for faithful diligent study and the will to succeed through earnest and determinative effort.

We hope, that the example that has been set by this fine young woman will be an inspiration to young people not only in Orlando, but throughout Florida and the entire Southland.

Much credit is due Mrs. J. Mark Cox for her aggressive leadership and others of her faithful supporters and every well meaning citizen white or black. All led on by one of America's most progressive Mayors, the Honorable Robert (Bob) Carr who deserves much praise and thanks for his calm fearless leadership.

Many congratulations to Mrs. Ravenall and may you forever continue to be the beautiful humble Christian Lady that you are. God bless you.

Pauline as the Cover Girl

During my work experience, my coworkers were very understanding of me keeping Sabbath. During my transfer to the Engineering Department, the planning director suggested that I move my belongings on Friday because he knew that I would not be there on Saturday with the moving crew. He was right. He had learned that, as a Seventh-day Adventist, I would not be there. This support could also be because Dr. Elaine Cox (who was an SDA) was on the Mayor's Committee.

I continued my education, enrolling in vocational classes, and then enrolling in Rollins College in Winter Park, Florida, a suburb of Orlando.

Ignorance is a terrible thing because for five years I attended vocational classes, not understanding the difference between vocational certificates and college degrees. I had no mentor. I could have been a long way into my educational desires had I known. The late Ruth Bracy-Stokes became my mentor. She explained the difference between vocational classes and college classes. A petite, friendly lady, she was very helpful as I began my college studies. She was a well-known Christian lady. I never heard a negative word about her. She possessed Christian values. She was my best friend.

During the period from 1960–1971, I had the privilege of serving as church clerk at Mt. Sinai SDA Church in Orlando, Florida, under Pastors Frank Stokes, J.H. Lawrence, T.M. Fountain, C. Dunbar Henri, Ralph Franklin, Gerald Wells, and James Best. My duties included attending all church board and business meetings, preparing church bulletins, attending funerals, reading aloud all church announcements during Sabbath services, and recording new baptisms.

In 1970, I began to attend Valencia Community College. I was seeking an AA degree in Business Administration. Now that I understood the difference between vocational classes and college degrees, I was ready to learn more about this new-found world of academic, college-level education! I dove into my classes and took as many business administration and management classes as I could.

Norris was a provider for our family. He was very quiet, non-talkative, only if it was necessary. His children were his priority. He enjoyed just being with them and playing sports and watching sports with them on TV. Norris was an only child. He believed in cleanliness and always made sure the children were clean, even brushing their hair before sending them out to play. He was clean and neat in his appearance. He was content spending time at home. Norris was not a public Seventh-day Adventist, but he was a believer in his heart. He never interfered with my time spent with my church obligations. Norris passed away unexpectedly in December of 1971 with a cerebral hemorrhage following an accident while changing a tire on one of our vehicles, leaving me to care for three dependent children on a $65/weekly salary with all the expenses of a homeowner. He was only forty-seven.

Norris had always kept records of his yearly employment information and would always say if something happened to him, I should take the papers to his job, and I would be given his due benefits. Soon after his death, I followed his instructions, only to find out that the papers did not have my name on them as beneficiary. Therefore, I had to hire a legal firm of attorneys. I had no knowledge of the legal system and felt totally lost. A year later, I learned that the court ruled not in my favor; therefore, I had to submit to the appellate court. After waiting for another year, I received what was left after attorney fees and court cost.

God is faithful. I had prayed that if the Lord blessed, I would send a donation to Oakwood College for a worthy student addressed to Dr. Calvin Rock—the president. He was the only person I knew there. My parents never used government assistance with us; therefore, I never used it with my family. God has always provided. My children were enrolled in the SDA school system at Orlando Junior Academy and Forest Lake Academy in Forest City, Florida, where they completed their studies.

CHAPTER 5

In 1970, the assistant city engineer, along with other officials, was seeking an African American name to be placed in a new Richmond Estates subdivision, along with other named professionals and well-known blacks, and my name was selected because of my civic duties in the community. Ravenall Street and Ravenall Park located in Richmond Estates, Southwest Section of Orlando. This street and park are still named after me today.

Pauline Ravenall On The Map

City Hall's Pauline Ravenall has joined the distinguished group of citizens that includes such personages as former Mayors Summerlin, Davis and Marks, athletic great Willie Mays, and the late jazz pianist Nat King Cole.

Mrs. Ravenall, of the Engineering Department, has had an Orlando street named after her. Ravenall Avenue is located in Richmond Heights, seventh addition, part of a 1,000-home subdivision off Kirkman Road in West Orlando, near the Ravenall home.

Pauline Ravenall

Officials of Federal Construction Co., Richmond Heights developers, were at a loss for appropriate street names when they presented the plot for the new addition to Engineering. Ralph Singleton, chief of Engineering's Plans and Survey section, suggested one be named Ravenall in honor of her fine civic and job records.

Mrs. Ravenall, mother of a daughter, 13, and two sons, 10 and 8, has worked for the City since July, 1964. She is active in the Seventh Day Adventist Church and, during her evening and spare hours, is working toward a Business Administration degree.

She has completed two and a half years at Rollins and Valencia Junior colleges.

Mrs. Ravenall's husband, Norris, is a foreman with Harry P. Leu Inc., Orlando.

Street and Park Are Named for Pauline Ravenall

After being employed for more than ten years as a clerical worker, having trained other employees, and done my best, the then-city-engineer—without considering me for a newly created position—placed a female Caucasian employee into the new position, which I trained into the position. I asked why I was not considered; his reply was, "I did not think you were interested." I immediately took leave of absence to finish my classwork at Valencia College where I completed by Associate's Degree in Business Administration. After my one-year leave of absence, I returned to my desk, typed a resignation letter to the engineer, and left my secretarial position and my position as a police officer reservist.

Pauline Receiving Farewell Gift from Ralph Singleton, Assistant City Engineer, and Staff

Soon thereafter, in September of 1975, I secured a house for purchase in Huntsville, Alabama. Looking for a fresh start, I went to continue my education at Alabama A&M University and to enroll my children into Oakwood Academy. I rented a U-Haul®, placed what I could in it, along with my dependent children and dog, locked my doors to my house (I decided to keep my house in Florida), and drove to Huntsville, Alabama.

I enrolled my children in Oakwood Academy, and I enrolled in Alabama A&M University. During the years from 1975–1977, I received a notice from the mortgage company that my house I purchased in Alabama was in foreclosure. The real estate agent had not been completely clear in the transaction, and I needed to get clear title to ownership. Apparently, either intentionally or unintentionally, someone at the real estate company failed in their duties to provide the necessary property search by a licensed title company that is required to show that there are no encumbrances from legal ownership.

I knew no one except Pastor C.B. Rock, the then-president of Oakwood College. I went to see him and told him my situation. He was kind and suggested that I contact Pastor E.C. Ward. I went to see Pastor Ward. He said for me to get an attorney and that I "was about to lose everything that I owned." He knew the character and background of the real estate agent that negotiated for me in purchasing my home in Alabama. For two years (1975–1977), I attended classes full time, earning a BS Degree in Business Administration. I graduated May 1977. The attorney that I contacted had previous business dealings with this same agent and knew him. The attorney made the phone contact as we—me, my sister, and brother-in-law—sat in his office and demanded that a clear title of property be in his office within thirty days. The demand was met. Therefore, I obtained clear title to my property and remained until I sold it in 1978.

I departed Huntsville in September of 1977. The summer of 1977, I attended camp meeting in Hawthorne, Florida. There I met the late Pastor R.L. Woolfork (conference president) and the late Pastor Robert Patterson (treasurer of the South Atlantic Conference). There, I was offered a secretarial position in education in the conference office in Atlanta, Georgia. Even though I wasn't looking for a job after not working for more than two years, I needed a job. I attended A&M University non-stop for two years. I had also been offered a job at A&M University. I really liked living in Huntsville, with no desire to move to Atlanta. Family members and I made it a matter of prayer for a decision, stating whoever called me first is the one I would accept. The next morning, Pastor Robert Patterson called first. As I was talking with him, the person from A&M called. Even though I desired to remain in Huntsville, my promise to God I had to keep.

A few weeks later in October of 1977, I was moved to Atlanta, Georgia, to begin my work as secretary in the Education Department at the South Atlantic Conference.

I thought working in the conference office with fellow Christians would somehow place me a little closer to the kingdom—not so! I was sadly mistaken. May I inject here: "Living with saints in heaven that will be glory. Living with saints on earth, that's another story." I just tried to maintain and stay focused. You know the verse, "For where two or three are gathered together in my name, there am I in the midst of them." (Matt. 18:20)? Unfortunately HE is not always in their midst. I just had to keep doing my job and living the life HE would want me to live and be the example HE would want me to give.

The late Elder G. Heflin Taylor (the Sabbath school director for the conference) was a man of great discernment. On several occasions, when he would come into the office, he could observe my anxiety, and he would say, "Come, Pauline. Let's have prayer in my office." He was a great man. The late President Robert L. Woolfork was gracious.

During my work at the conference, I was privileged to travel to parts unknown on tours throughout Europe: Italy, England, Africa, Holy Land, and many others. So, after my two years at South Atlantic Conference (1977–1979), I left the conference.

In 1979, I became employed with the state of Georgia Education Department, located in Atlanta, Georgia. In 1978, I had enrolled in Atlanta University to study Public Administration. After one term of studying, I became disinterested and weary with studying and working, thereby ending my studies. I just needed a break from it all.

Two years later, I began working as a claim examiner with the federal government in the Department of Defense (Ft. McPherson Military Installation) in Atlanta, Georgia. After five years, I applied and was accepted in the Diversion Program at FBI Headquarters in Quantico, Virginia, as the diversion investigator for pharmaceutical drugs. I was trained in the process of investigating illegal drugs and pharmaceutical drugs and be able to identify the difference between them. My undercover police work had initially prepared me for the training, but the position was short-lived because of my commitment to my Lord and Savior to observe the Sabbath.

In 1981, I remembered how I enjoyed law enforcement with the Orlando Police Department as an undercover officer. I went to the Atlanta Police Department, was interviewed, and was about to be assigned to a unit. I confessed that according to the policies of the department I was older than the law required. The application was cancelled.

Soon thereafter, I learned about the paralegal profession. A lawyer friend suggested that I contact John Marshall, a private law school. After my interview, I enrolled and completed the six-month program—nonstop.

With certification in hand, I decided to check out the Judicial Law Program. Following my interview with the owner, I was told that he would need my LSAT scores. I arranged for testing for the LSAT to comply with school requirements to enter the program. I was approved for admission but soon discovered that there is a big difference between judicial law and civil law. Because I like a challenge, I stayed with it. And after three years of non-stop studying, in May of 1995, I graduated with a Doctor of Jurisprudence Degree.

Pauline Graduating from Law School

To this day, I remember how I felt the last day of class. I said if I had to attend class one more day, I would just sit down on the classroom floor and cry! I was totally exhausted. During my years of study, I maintained my own six-bed state-licensed personal care home with four to five patients in my care, in addition to working eight to nine hours a day for the Internal Revenue Service for the entire time I was in school.

I was thankful for my education and the hard work I put into becoming a lawyer. I have had many experiences that I would not have had otherwise. At one point I was able to meet the renowned attorney Johnny Cochran at an event in Detroit, Michigan, where he was the keynote speaker. We met after his presentation. He was very kind and gracious and encouraged me to "come on out here with them—they needed me."

Pauline and Attorney Johnny Cochran

In 1998, while employed with IRS, I became restless and needed a diversion from my routine. As I was visiting Mt. Sinai SDA Church on a Sabbath, Pastor Calvin B. Rock was preaching and extended an invitation to become involved with Operation ReachBack. He explained the process. Upon returning home to Atlanta, I learned of a planned trip by ORB to travel to Ethiopia, East Africa.

> *That was one of the most challenging and heartbreaking missions that I had ever experienced. I cried most of the time. I became known, or at least referred to, as the "the crying lady."*

I was at work, sitting at my desk, and thought this was my diversion opportunity! I left my desk, went to the manager's desk and said to her: "I need to take time off." Matter of fact, it was Memorial Day weekend. I requested time off—without pay. Within minutes, the requested time was approved.

I made all necessary arrangements, connected with the group coordinator, and flew to Addis Ababa, East Africa, arriving at nighttime —not knowing anyone from the group. I was met at the airport by Dr. Edwards. We had never met. He was holding up a sign asking each passerby, "Are you Pauline Ravenall?" He even asked a Caucasian female that was just ahead of me. She responded: "No." Once we met, I was taken to my living quarters to begin our mission assignment.

That was one of the most challenging and heartbreaking missions that I had ever experienced. I cried most of the time. I became known, or at least referred to, as the "the crying lady." Our first stop was at the Gimbi Health Clinic, about a day's journey from Addis Ababa. Arriving there, we found no medications for the sick and injured. There was a gentleman representing Loma Linda Medical Center who had shipped medical supplies for Gimbi Health Clinic, but it had not arrived. He thought that because a war was going on in another area, the supplies were diverted to the war area. One patient was lying on an uncovered plastic mattress with insects flying around, an IV drip in his arm. So sad. I mentioned to our leader that I could send sheets to cover the beds. He responded, "They need more than sheets here." And it was obvious that they did.

We also visited a college in another city to assess its needs. We found that there were few necessary supplies for the students to use. Each team member was asked to select a personal project from the list provided. I selected a VCR. It took several months to discover if it had been received by the college once I returned home and mailed the VCR to the conference office address. After many inquiries, the package was discovered in the conference office, unopened—just sitting there. There were also group projects to provide such as moped bikes for the pastors to travel to their churches and farming equipment.

Gimbi, Ethiopia, in East Africa

On April 30, 2000, I retired from my job with the IRS as a claim adjuster for business accounts. I had been an employee of the civil service with the federal government for more than nineteen years. I could have continued working but desired to leave for parts unknown!

CHAPTER 6

In July 2000, I was invited to accept a missionary assignment as an ESL (English as a second language) teacher in Seoul, South Korea. Orientation to Asian culture was held in Hong Kong, China. I arrived in Seoul in September 2000 via Hong Kong, China, to begin my teaching experience. It was not difficult for me to adjust to a new culture. The food preparation was a little different than I was used to, but the food was healthy and delicious. Maybe it was because of the natural herbs and seasonings or fresh ingredients. Maybe it was because food was steamed or slow cooked with less oil. I never learned to prepare food in this way myself, but I always enjoyed partaking and especially I enjoyed experiencing a new culture.

Teachers and Students Receiving Certifications, Seoul, South Korea

After working six months with no illness or any problems, I suddenly became ill. In retrospect, I believe it was a result of my eating six scoops of Baskin-Robbins® ice cream and popcorn. It was during Christmas break. Most of the foreign teachers had returned to their country, but I remained at the school alone. I bought a television set to have something do and decided to walk to the store and bought and ate ice cream. A few days later, I felt lethargic. No pain. I just could not sit or stand. The coordinator suggested to the pastor to get me to a doctor. He did. After examination, the doctor suggested I be taken to a hospital. The pastor and elder placed me in the car, with me lying in the back seat, traveling three to four hours to the Sahmyook Seventh-day Adventist Hospital in Seoul, South Korea. By this time, I had collapsed into a diabetic coma. I had diabetes without knowing it.

> *I remained in a coma for five days—Monday through Sabbath. The administration and teachers had come to visit, left get well cards, and prayed for me. My family had tried to reach me—all this was unknown to me.*

I remained in a coma for five days—Monday through Sabbath. The administration and teachers had come to visit, left get well cards, and prayed for me. My family had tried to reach me—all this was unknown to me. But on Sabbath, my bedside phone rang, the Holy Spirit awakened me—my son Kevin was on the phone. *Thank You, Lord!* What a happy conversation that was! My coworker (Azure), a Korean and former missionary teacher, spoke English and had been beside my bed to translate to the Korean doctors. I asked why she was there. She said she asked permission to come translate for me.

I was confined in the hospital for more than a week. The doctors were not sure of my situation and suggested that I be returned to the United States. My son Kevin (in Atlanta) was the one to come and assist me. He had to secure an urgent passport. He contacted Cynthia McKinney, a senator from my home state of Georgia. She was a US congresswoman and an African-American representative's officer and sworn to respond when there was an urgent need, but she never did. We had to turn our efforts elsewhere.

Students in the Classroom, Seoul, South Korea

There were only two scheduled flights from Atlanta to Seoul during that week. Therefore, Kevin had to arrange to make reservation to get on one of the flights without knowing how or when he was going to get his emergency passport. Then he reached out to Representative Max Cleland and within a few hours, he traveled to the state of Louisiana to get his passport, and with passport and ticket in hand, he arrived in Seoul to escort me back to the States.

I returned to the United States to seek medical help. After my short stay back home in Atlanta, I returned to Seoul to continue my teaching in a different province. I praise the Lord continually for His blessings, that where HE leads, He gives me the courage to follow.

Teachers were encouraged to take breaks away from the classroom. The teaching schedule was classes went from 6:00 a.m. to noon and then again from 6:00 p.m. to 10:00 p.m. Most teachers taught six to eight classes per day. On Friday, classes ended at noon and vespers was at 7 p.m. On Sabbath morning at 10:00, there were various programs, then at 11:00, there was the divine service. Lunch was always provided for the entire church membership. In the afternoon, there were Bible classes or other religious activities. Occasionally, outreach ministries were scheduled.

Because it was a busy and rigorous schedule, the admin encouraged teachers to take breaks. While working in Korea, I took a break and visited Vietnam.

From November 2006 to November 2007, I took a break to work with Pastor C.B. Rock in a revival meeting held by the late Pastor E.E. Cleveland, in Las Vegas, Nevada. Pastor Rock assigned Sr. Velvet Richey to assist me in making contact with former members to invite them to the meetings. At the end of the crusade, there was a baptism, and many souls accepted Christ as their Savior and were united with the church through baptism into the Abundant Life Seventh-day Adventist Church.

Sr. Ellen Clark was one of the new candidates. She is still very active in the church, and a close associate with sister Richie.

The Bible workers consisted of Carolyn Hinson, Bobby Andrews, the late Rosa Jones, Derick Germany, Pauline Ravenall.

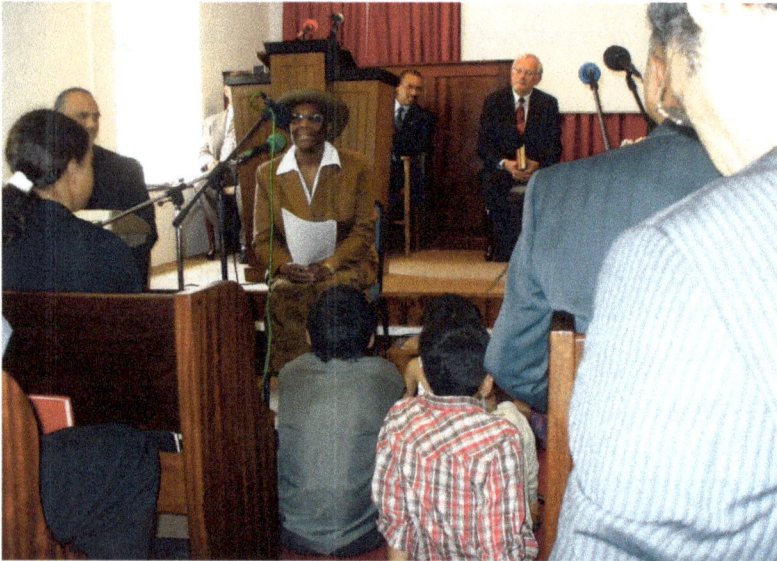

SDA Church (Children story) on the Island of St. Helena, in the South Atlantic Ocean, the Home of Napoleon Bonaparte (French Military Ruler, 1804–1815)

After returning to Korea and teaching for another year following this break, I was invited to attend the sixty-year anniversary of the Adventist church on the island of St. Helena (the homeland of Napoleon Bonaparte). I was housed at Heidelberg International College in Cape Town, South Africa, for a few days until the ship arrived to transport me to St. Helena. I visited with students and attended chapel services on campus. I departed from Cape Town, South Africa, after touring Robben Island where Nelson Mandela was imprisoned for twenty-seven years. My journey would take seven days with only one stop to board other passengers. Once on the island, we did missionary work for a Voice of Prophecy meeting, which concluded with the mayor and other diplomats from the island in attendance. There were approximately eighty-five plus passengers on the cargo ship which included eight invitees for the church participations from South Africa.

After working as a missionary for nearly ten years, living and working in various provinces throughout South Korea, I returned to the United States in June of 2010 in time to attend the General Conference Session in Atlanta. (Since my first General Conference experience, I had only missed one since 1965 [Atlantic City, New Jersey] with my best friend, the late Ruth Stokes, and my sister, the late Bernice Barnes-Powell.)

Stan and Jan (Husband and Wife), Director and Teacher, Almise SDA School in Vlore, Albania

A few months later (February 2011), I was asked to replace a husband-wife team of teachers in Vlore, Albania. I consented. I traveled to Albania to teach ESL (English as a second language). I taught junior high students and adults for special preparations training. The pastor/teacher (Stan Hendrickson) and a church member picked me up from the airport in Tirana, the capital city of Albania—a three-hour journey. Stan Hendrickson is the director of the Almise SDA school in Vlore, Albania. He is the all-around person at the facility. He had been there for more than fourteen years before I arrived, and he still remains on board there. He is a man of Christ from the heart. I lived and worked there in Vlore for a little less than a year. The husband and teacher was the director, pastor, all-around repairman, and community activist. As I was told by Stan, during his fourteen years in Vlore, I was the first black he had seen during his stay in Vlore. It was thought that I was a spy.

As I prepared to leave Albania, I traveled to Greece and had hopes to visit Athens, but because of the unrest there at the time, my visit to Greece was cut short.

In 2013, I became restless for something to do. I reached out to the International Language School to assist immigrants to receive their permanent citizenship. I volunteered at the school for about five years assisting students to qualify for U.S. citizenship. Students were required to learn and to know the U.S. Constitution well enough to answer in the affirmative to pass and receive their citizenship. The subjects were taught in English, but provisions are made for students that did not speak or understand English fluently enough to answer the questions at the ceremony. I learned much by assisting the students with their training. This I have done until the present time (2019) with only occasional breaks away from the classroom.

May I introduce the late Clara Peterson Rock? She was the wife of the former vice president of the General Conference, Calvin B. Rock. She is well-known throughout the Adventist denomination. Her husband Calvin was a former president of Oakwood College/University in Huntsville, Alabama. Her father, Frank L. Peterson, was one of the pioneers of the early Adventist church and a former president of Oakwood. In 2010 Oakwood University opened the Clara Peterson Rock Museum in the Eva B. Dykes Library to recognize her contributions to the university and education. This special section of the library on the first floor contains the black SDA historical materials that she gathered and organized as a display for visitors to learn more about the legacy of black Seventh-day Adventists. This display is named after her. I believe she will be known and remembered by some, if not most.

In the earlier years, before Mrs. Clara P. Rock's health began to decline. We had shared some time together. Thereafter, when Pastor Rock required assistance, they both agreed and asked if I would assist with her care. I consented and was pleased to do so. For a few years, we shared many pleasant days and weeks together. First thing in the morning, she read her Bible. Then she would ask what was for breakfast. She seemed to have had a hearty appetite. We always shared snacks together. In earlier times, we would go shopping together. She did not like being outside. Therefore, we would watch television. She liked to sing. Occasionally, she would play the piano and sing. I have very fond memories of her and the kindness they both shared with me. She had many favorites TV programs: Oakwood University services (especially the Aeolians) and Red Foxx (comedy). She always enjoyed playing her musical tapes.

Thus concludes my story. I am amazed and grateful at how the Lord has led me from the plantation to the courts of mediation and all over the world telling others about His love.

In 2016, I enrolled and completed a certified nursing assistant (CNA) program to continue assisting those who are in need of personal care. The training helped me to better assist with Mrs. Rock's care.

Thus concludes my story. I am amazed and grateful at how the Lord has led me from the plantation through the courts to mediation and all over the world telling others about His love. I am thankful to the Lord that I can still make a difference in the lives of others. Looking back over my life, it is clear that a divine hand was guiding me every step of my journey. I've had ups and I've had downs, but I know that God was with me through every twist and turn. My interest has always been seeking ways that might help someone with a need and God has blessed me beyond measure. Presently I hold a Georgia property and casualty license, a

Georgia claims adjusters license, and am a licensed mediator in the state of Georgia. I would like to be of assistance wherever I can, even for the least of these. I often reflect on how much I was in need of legal help after my husband passed. Now, I wish to CONTINE HELPING, with God's blessing, whenever the need arises.

Mediation—The Ravenall Dispute Resolution Services

My hope is that you, dear reader, will be inspired and uplifted by my story. I pray that you will keep pursuing the path that God has for you. I pray that you will follow His leading, and one day soon, may we all meet in heaven.

TEACH Services, Inc.
P U B L I S H I N G

We invite you to view the complete
selection of titles we publish at:
www.TEACHServices.com

We encourage you to write us
with your thoughts about this,
or any other book we publish at:
info@TEACHServices.com

TEACH Services' titles may be purchased in
bulk quantities for educational, fund-raising,
business, or promotional use.
bulksales@TEACHServices.com

Finally, if you are interested in seeing
your own book in print, please contact us at:
publishing@TEACHServices.com
We are happy to review your manuscript at no charge.